WISDOM'S GAME

How to Change Life's Pain Into Joy

✦★✦

*Judi Thomases
And the Brotherhood
Of Light Workers*

**FLESH PUBLIC LIBRARY
124 W. GREENE ST.
PIQUA, OH 45356-2399**

Cypress House

WISDOM'S GAME:
How to Change Life's Pain Into Joy
Copyright © 2005 by Judi Thomases

All rights reserved. This book may not be reproduced in whole or in part, by any means, electronic or mechanical, without prior written permission from the publisher. For information, or to order additional copies of this book, please contact:

Cypress House
155 Cypress Street
Fort Bragg, CA 95437
(800) 773-7782
www.cypresshouse.com
To contact the author visit www.WisdomsGame.com

Disclaimer

We have made every effort to attribute the sources of quotes and stories. If items have no attribution, either we couldn't determine the source or these items were written by the author. We appreciate hearing from readers who can identify the sources of any unattributed items.

Cover Design: Elizabeth Petersen

Library of Congress Cataloging-in-Publication Data

Thomases, Judi, 1941-
  Wisdom's game : how to change life's pain into joy / by Judi Thomases and the Brotherhood of Light Workers.
    p. cm.
  ISBN 1-879384-57-4 (pbk. : alk. paper)
  1. Wisdom. 2. Suffering. I. Brotherhood of Light Workers. II. Title.
  BF1999.T513 2004
  299'.93--dc22   2004012097

Printed in the USA
2 4 6 8 9 7 5 3 1

To my husband, Carl R. Cacioppo, Jr.,
who has always been my rock and foundation
and who encouraged me in every phase of
my work to bring these messages to everyone.

Spirit is playing a game.

The game is that the world is you, and you are the world!

What does that mean?
How does it feel?

How can the game be won?

Contents

Acknowledgments ix
About the Author xi
Foreword xv
Section One – Wisdom's Game: The Messages . . 1
   1. The Beginning 3
   2. Suffering Is Spirit's Game 7
   3. Smallness and Limitation 11
   4. Finishing the Game 15
   5. Perfecting the Universe through the Computer . . . 19
   6. The Five Rules 23
   7. The First Order of Business 27
   8. New Desires 33
   9. Types of Wisdom 37
   10. Soul Choices 41
   11. Three Easy Steps 45
   12. Fear, Pain, and Sorrow 49
   13. Despair is A Faulty Notion 53

14. Conscious Design	57
15. The Journey Home	61
16. Duality's Paradox	65
17. Straight to Bliss	69
18. Consciousness: The Other Realm	73
19. Humanity's Mandate	77
20. The Journey through Form	81
21. The End of Time and The Beginning of Wholeness	85
Postscript	89
SECTION TWO – RECAP OF MESSAGES	97
Previews Revisited	99
The Five Rules	105
ORDER FORM	107

Acknowledgments

First and foremost, I must offer my deepest gratitude to the discarnate teaching entities who call themselves The Brotherhood of Light Workers, for choosing me as a vehicle for their transmissions and trusting me with the task of conveying their message to the world. As this book could not have come into being without that interchange between our two realms, I must also give gratitude to all the gurus, spiritual masters, and occult tutors who led me over many years down the path toward wisdom and receptivity, and who taught me the basics of meditation so that ultimately I could be receptive to "the small still voice within."

My deepest thanks go to my friend, Sheryl Leach, whom I consider a twin fragment of the same oversoul group, and who has been muse for the undertaking of this book as well as advisor and backer of the project. She has not only remained a firm believer in the power of the Brotherhood's teachings, but has also roused in my heart the enthusiasm to press on with this mission no matter the hurdles.

My husband, Carl Cacioppo, has been my touchstone, informal editor, and constant loving support system throughout the effort, never refusing me his opinion but always encouraging my attempts. My son, Andrew Thomases, has been my legal counselor, with whose support many business considerations were easily and successfully concluded. And my daughter, Holly Williams, has offered many suggestions on realizing the practical applications and publicizing the work.

I also want to thank Mike Flynn, my friend, fellow aspirant and *Seth* aficionado, and publisher of the former *Writings on the Wall* magazine, who started me on this published channelings path; Mahesh Grossman, my editor and spiritual mirror, whose similarity of path allowed him to see exactly what was needed to shape the material into its ideal form while maintaining the purity of that which was relayed; Simon Warwick-Smith, whose passion for spiritual guidance motivated him to share with me his knowledge of the publishing business and other insights; fellow channeler and author Alice Kann, who generously shared her advice and previous experience; and Joyce Critelli and Michael Jonat, friends, clients, and spiritual seekers, whose enthusiasm and curiosity brought forth many stellar messages from the Brotherhood.

About the Author

I have always been psychic to a degree. At twenty-one I had what can only be called a reincarnational or reawakened memory. My abilities really blossomed when I reached age thirty-three. Many powerful examples of ESP occurred over several years, finally propelling me to find my calling as a spiritual counselor and astrologer.

For the next twenty-three years, I saw clients as a consultant in astrology, Tarot, metaphysics, and intuitive sciences. I taught, lectured at conventions and seminars, made radio and TV appearances, and wrote articles. By receiving information from sources such as Tarot cards, AstroDice, and I Ching, I specialized in psychologically oriented spiritual guidance for important life choices. Meanwhile, as an avid scholar and a Phi Beta Kappa, I began a lifelong study of paths of spiritual growth including Yoga, Eastern philosophies, Sufi dance, Kabbalah, the Major Arcana, and the Hermetic Mystery School teachings. Also, I explored certain self-discovered abilities such as a natural sensitivity to perceiving higher vibrational energy fields, both visually and through the astral body's electromagnetic sphere. I have helped people heal their physical bodies, and passed along insights about the emotional causes of their various ailments.

I became the founder of a women's spiritual network for meditation, teaching, and personal development; director and founder of monthly gatherings for spiritual/metaphysical understanding; director and founder of an interdisciplinary self-development center, and board member of a networking group for holistic practitioners.

But nothing could have prepared me for the event that took place in January 1997.

I was at my desk, writing in my journal, when a string of words entered my awareness, loud as can be for silent reception, and gave me exactly the guidance I needed for everything that was bothering me at that moment! *"A game,"* it said. *"Life's a game. Remember. You're stuck in jail. Find the Go-Free escape card! We will help."*

What?! *Who* will help? Who's talking in my head?

It was a very disconcerting experience.

The inner voice continued: *"You will hear us more clearly soon. Keep tuning in. The psi or spiritual is widening. Just work on that for now. This is a new talent you are unfolding. You are light! Beautiful, clear light! In the darkest hour, place, or thought, you can hear this/our voice—we'll light the way. Later, you can use the path, the way, the light to help others. We are Love. It's easy. Ask questions. You are opening up… we are glad to receive you. It will keep flowing, ever more. You have arrived, finally! Bye for now."*

This was quite an encounter to assimilate, but I was already familiar with the concept of channeling, and was able to accept its reality, take its guidance into my life, and ultimately use its messages to heal others. With one step leading to another, that's how I became a channel for the group entity calling itself The Brotherhood of Light Workers.

That amazing and fascinating penetration of other realms has transformed my work and increased my clientele and readership. My efforts in relaying the words of my spirit guides, showing an empowering new way to view life's hardships, have resulted in many heartfelt testimonials from clients, publishers, and colleagues. The material I have received has been published as a monthly column, as a proto-book, *The Curriculum For Handling Earth-School*, and incorporated into articles that have appeared in national magazines. These teachings have caused me to rename my work Wisdom Path Guidance, for that's what it has become.

*The Best Description I've Found of
What I Do as a Channeler:*

"Channeling was once the preserve of 19th century mediums who claimed to be able to communicate with the spirits of the dead, often via a control spirit. Although mediums are still with us, they have since been joined by a wide variety of other people who claim to be able to channel disembodied entities including many modern UFO cults....

"Channeling differs from the previously discussed examples because the mediums have a degree of control over the phenomenon they exhibit and also because the personalities themselves often do not 'possess' the whole body but instead *relay messages to the medium who then relays them to the sitters.*" [Italics mine.]

— Paul Chambers, "First Person Plural,"
(*Fortean Times,* Jan. 2000)

Foreword

I first became acquainted with the messages of the Brotherhood of Light Workers through Judi's contributions to a small magazine called *Writings on the Wall*, which explored a variety of channelings both current and past. Naturally, such a forum fit my late wife Jane Roberts' offerings—the Seth material—so that each month for many years I enjoyed receiving and reading new issues.

I was immediately struck by the depth of wisdom conveyed in the brotherhood's messages, and by their similarity in essence to some of Seth's teachings. Seth, and the entities calling themselves the Brotherhood of Light Workers, and others like them, appear to have been assigned the task of communicating hidden truths about life and proposing a new perspective for us to see the world. But for these assignments to be completed successfully, certain people have to serve as receivers, and since these transmissions are conducted non-verbally and non-tangibly, such receivers must be mediumistically gifted. I'd say the mark of talent in this is in how clearly the messages are heard and put forth so that the reader or listener can easily understand what's being taught. Judi's gift is apparent in these pages. The new ideas coming across are as unmistakable as they are enlightening.

It's my sincere hope that the reader enjoys this book as any of Jane's Seth works, and takes from it the insights and understanding that bring peace and open the heart.

Robert Butts, Husband of late author
Jane Roberts ("Seth"), Sayre, PA

Wisdom's Game

How to Change Life's Pain Into Joy

"But this swift business I must uneasy make, lest too light winning make the prize light."
— William Shakespeare, *The Tempest* (Prospero)

"Good judgment comes from experience, and a lot of that comes from bad judgment."
— Attributed to Will Rogers

Section One

Wisdom's Game
The Messages

To laugh at yourself in the midst of your gloom is the best possible antidote to heal the sting of pain.

One

THE BEGINNING

Preview: Wisdom teaches that, while temporary pain is normal, continual suffering over its cause isn't necessary. We can instantly change our thoughts to take things more lightly.

In fact, there is a beginning; we have already spoken of it.*
A beginning is the point after which everything else flows, the trigger for whatever else is to come.

A new start has begun, and it is called the voice of spirit.† It has no embodiment, and so it will be called Wisdom. It has no face, but a generalized voice that will speak to your readers about what is fitting to learn and perceive, and also what is foolish to dwell upon.

The voice, Wisdom, has several essential points to make. It wishes the world to become more alive and more aligned. It is the path to that end.

Wisdom cannot tell you exactly what to create out of your life; doing so would eliminate the need to live. Wisdom can only aid or guide you in creating your world. Wisdom has learned all it knows from the very method you are using—trial and error, live or die, succeed or fail. Wisdom has not come into itself by an elevated route that's above it all. Instead, it has come to its knowing in the same step-by-step way. Only, having gotten immeasurably farther along the path than you are right now, it can speak to you as though you were a student, conveying knowledge as you travel, attempting to reach the inner mind with words that echo truth, and with guidance that feels inwardly or intuitively correct.

Wisdom wants to tell everyone that there is no need to

---

* This reference is to one of the earliest received messages, given on January 23, 1997, in which Genesis is described as everyone's story of inception (i.e., the idea of Genesis isn't just of the world; it's of each of us. Since we each create or initiate the world, "Genesis" means that each person creates his or her own world as well).

† This voice, also known as The Brotherhood of Light Workers, is also identifying itself herein as Wisdom.

suffer. It is a big lesson for humankind. Suffering is a dilemma. Truth for the individual can only be known or gotten by trial and error. The "error" part describes a period of pain. How can this be avoided when there really is no shortcut through the process?

We do not say that painful lessons don't exist or aren't necessary—we say that the suffering caused by such mistakes can be easily alleviated by a new awareness.

Awakening into oneself recalls a baby who is born through a long, painful delivery, and who may continue to cry after arriving here. The continued crying is neither the shock of air nor the smack of hand on rump, but the reaction to the long struggle, and is thus an unnecessary continuation of suffering.

You are all like that until you learn to grow and change. The process whereby you learn right from wrong and good from bad—always the way of the world—is difficult, but then there is finality. After that, continued suffering is your own choice, however unconscious.

Wisdom wants to bring it all into consciousness. Wisdom wants you to have the best tools to fight the darkness encompassing so many lives, and show how the Elevated Ones react to their lessons and struggles.

Above all, Wisdom tells you that it's okay to hurt—temporarily—but then it's wise to move on. Moving on entails moving into joy and glory and out of pain as quickly as humanly possible.

How fast can that be? Instantaneous! Wisdom knows the truth of this: to laugh at yourself in the midst of your gloom is the best possible antidote to heal the sting of pain, and banishes suffering as fast as thought.

We are at the point of completing this first thought. As our beginning, and as your introduction to spirit's voice, know that all we will say will affect your energy body, and that by allowing these ideas to penetrate the dense layers of your self—your body's defenses as well as your mind's resistance—you will begin to change, utterly and wonderfully, in your real being. You will swallow Wisdom into your gut, and find that it works like a blossom to expand and open deep, impenetrable layers, and awaken your own inner voice of spirit. We will reconnect the dots. You will brighten and develop the inner beauty you know is there, masked by so much history and encumbrance. We will sing your "body electric" and dance your molecules alive! Thank you for accepting these teachings, and know thyself as a brand-new student, or acolyte, on the path of joy.

Every form in nature... has the very same experience: to journey from one state to another... to experience a certain amount of struggle until reaching a perfected state....

Two

SUFFERING IS SPIRIT'S GAME

Preview: You are spirit inside matter—this trick required the sacrifice of knowing your real power. You okayed this for one reason: to learn wisdom. There's only one way to get to it: to accept suffering, which is the gift that turns pure but boring spiritual existence into challenging and purposeful life. The struggle of growing is what life's all about. Enjoy it!

If there is one thing for all to recognize, it is that there is no real division between our differing realms, for while we are everywhere, so you are, too.

You have disguised your true nature by veiling it in the cloak of form. You have chosen this to gain experiences whereby to conquer the unknowns of your nature—also called your truth—and to do so, you had to shrink downward, into matter, thereby attuning your energy or essence into a slower vibration and a heavier construction. Many things helped you do this, including the ability to inhabit dense structures (you call this matter) with your awareness—known as consciousness or mind. To inhabit these realms meant that you must deliberately forego some greater, grander knowledge of existence and of your very being. To make this sacrifice, you had to leave a certain awareness and accept a kind of illusory reality that allowed you to know a part of yourself without knowing all of you.

Why would you want to make such a sacrifice? The answer is simple, and is what we talked about last: to learn Wisdom. Wisdom is the constant companion of such a journey, as well as the end goal. Wisdom, or shall we say the voice of experience, is the route you wished to take back into your most expanded being, known as spirit, or the divine part of life. It is a place of such wholeness and expansion that you might think there is nothing to it other than all-knowing wisdom. But that isn't so, for the state of spiritual being needs a journey through matter to learn what can be known by that; otherwise, it is only love and not the understanding born of pain.

You—as spirit, as God—wanted this journey with all your heart, and you waited your turn to accept a birth into it. You knew full well that you were saying yes to suffering—for that was the game. Suffering, and nothing else, is the abrasion that produces wisdom! It is hard but brilliant, like diamonds. It is a true gift, for without suffering you would float through everything, and nothing would have much meaning. Think of it! All life, an entire span of years, never feeling elation because you've never known despair; never feeling hurt because you've never known victory. Never feeling anything at all. What a drag!

You did not want that. It would have been the same as requesting—even praying for—eighty to ninety years of boredom. Ugh, we say!

We advise you to turn your attention now to another thought: if you did not experience all that being alive in a body holds, what would you strive for throughout existence? What would life's point be? We mean that spirit, as unformed, disembodied energy, would have no journey to make, no starting and ending points, and no path between them, if not for the built-in pain of living. The universe would collapse back upon itself, bereft of purpose, there to no avail.

Every form in nature, every thing that exists both to your perception and beyond, has the very same experience: to journey from one state to another, and while doing so, to experience a certain amount of struggle until reaching a perfected state, whereupon it can relax back into non-form or spirit. This holds true for bugs as well as people, and for planets, asteroids, and stars. The journey through states of being always holds the promise of experience, and within that, the joy of gaining wisdom. Make no mistake, it is ever so.

You have been journeying from the beginning of time, literally. You have tried a variety of forms: you have been mineral, then vegetable, then animal. You have been lower and higher animal. You finally reached humanhood, and you are still journeying, now toward a higher state, a state of advancing sentience. You are nowhere near complete, and are always gaining wisdom. Periodically, you have returned to disembodied stasis, an energy state between these trials, like a rest stop on your travels each lifetime.

We appreciate your ear, and will release it for now. We will resume again soon. In the meantime, be sure to give thanks sincerely for the gift you have received—not the gift of life, but the gift of suffering, for that's what will accompany all your chosen growth.

Amen.

*The reason that the soul chooses to live within a
constricted pattern, instead of vast and boundless,
is that there is more to play with when there
is smallness and limitation than when there is
hugeness and great empowerment.*

Three

SMALLNESS AND LIMITATION

Preview: Higher beings have needs too – primarily, to seek ever-deeper awareness. One of the best ways is to play the game of physical life. The rules of this game demand the acceptance of being small and limited. Smallness and limitation govern the physical universe, and are desirable strategies because their nature provides the richest field of experience.

There is another concept to be communicated: the reason that the soul chooses to live within a constricted pattern, instead of vast and boundless, is that there is more to play with when there is smallness and limitation than when there is hugeness and great empowerment. *The Gods are restless!*

Being Godlike is a state that can be enjoyed in only two forms: when one is not seeking anything outside oneself, or when one has found all there is to know about seeking. Obviously, these two positions are uncommon, and even Gods have needs—which is precisely why they play with becoming embodied and having the experiences of life.

For those of us who, in our quest, have passed beyond the need to play with small and limited forms, there is still the desire—need, you could say—to experience that which is no longer limitation, but is not yet all-ness, an intermediate state, lasting millennia, that allows us to grow farther and farther beyond. Here we can experiment with a partial Godhood, yet still be far removed from omnipotence and omniscience. It is a stage in the overall journey that you, too, will enjoy between and beyond the experience of living in a body.

We speak about smallness and limitation, a concept known to astrologers as Saturn, the lord of time, the lord of karma. It is the force that binds one within the encasement of time and space—in other words, the physical, three-dimensional universe that is all you can know, see, or realize while you are in your body. This force will hold you to its rules and tighten its grip on you if you wish to flee. It is the means by which you can know reality and within which you must accept its rules or limitations and learn from them. It is the most important force at work in the physical universe, for it is what will keep you physical, show you the pain of dealing with life as such, teach you the wisdom whence to grow, and encase you in its grip until you pass out of the universe—that is, die. It is a far stronger force for all physical beings than the force of gravity! Gravity binds you, but the lord of physical laws demands acknowledgment of itself in every moment, and will taunt you with its power until you wise up!

The symbol known as Saturn—or called the law of three-dimensionality—is the ruling agent of smallness and limitation; it is what allows you, as Godlike spirit, to become, and remain in, form. It has a mighty power, and must be well understood for you to walk through your journey here as lightly and comfortably as is allowed within the framework of life.

You are small, not because that is what defines you, but because you needed to be that so you could enjoy life.

You are bound, not because you are powerless, but because you needed to accept that before you could enjoy life.

In truth, you are neither, but you could not play the game of life without surrendering yourself to these two demands.

If and when the world itself changes, you can learn how to remain alive—that is, in a body—and expand beyond its constraints. The world shall become more permeable, and so shall you remember your true vastness and power. You shall learn to expand yourself in such a way that you can play with the very rules of physicality, and yet not die away from your body—thus leaving Saturn's realm. You shall grow farther than any human yet, and play with form, but never forsake the game that teaches wisdom and provides experience. You shall become Gods-as-human,[*] and the journey shall be the best yet!

---

[*] This is the true meaning of the Age of Aquarius!

You did not succumb to another, higher God in choosing to be part of this kind of game; you created it yourself, with the consent and cooperation of those who went before and were thus more experienced in taking part in what's called life.

Four

FINISHING THE GAME

Preview: Emotions are our albatross, but we willingly accepted their burden as the strategic challenge required to play the game of life, a game devised to cause growth. Up to now, we weren't aware that life was a game. But the basis of the Age of Aquarius is to remember our higher nature, our participation in this creation. The time has come – the "End Times" – to change the way the game is played. A new game is developing.

We are wondering about your issues regarding the times when hardships and delays trick you into despair. We want to discuss the emotions connected to these hard times, and how else a soul might respond to them.

In the beginning of humanity's journey, it was determined that you would always be subject to the sway of emotions, that in fact such reactive response would become the determining factor that defined humanity and distinguished you from the apes and other animals. Emotional responsiveness could then become both the determinant of sensitivity and compassion, but also the burden of life, for when it was out of balance and too overwhelming there would be real motivation to rediscover your wholeness. And so emotions would be the primary basis for human growth, even more than intellect. Those who would grow toward their spiritual attainment had best understand their own emotional reactions and learn mastery over them.

Furthermore, in case you were wondering, the creator of this plan was none other than yourselves. You did not succumb to another, higher God in choosing to be part of this kind of game; you created it yourself, with the consent and cooperation of those who went before and were thus more experienced in taking part in what's called life.

The reason for the choice is obvious: a game—plan to tackle and master something—must have tension, must have obstacle, and must have challenge. Otherwise, there's no point in playing. There must be a way to win, and in order to win over something, there must be some device that needs to be conquered. You exercised grand wisdom in devising such a choice, but then, once you entered the play, you completely forgot that you designed it so.

For what would be the point of it all if you knew or remembered the trick of winning while you were actually engaged in the ruse? You would instantly lose the main point of playing: to challenge your soul into growth.

So, let us repeat our point: you decided early on in the history of developing into humankind that you would deliberately play a game with your self, which would be to carry the difficult burden of emotional responsiveness into the act of being a physical being. You knew that this ploy meant life would get rough at times, and ecstatic at other times, and you said okay to participating because you knew that that way would allow you to increase your inner light through the challenge to survive, more than simple eating, sleeping, and reproducing would. You said okay to participating in the rules of the game, which included the rule that you must not remember who devised it and why you did so!

Now, a plateau has been reached, in which humanity is reawakening and remembering everything: who created the game, what the point of it all was, and where to go from here. It is a very exciting, alive time, and is named the Age of Aquarius. You are remembering yourself as God-in-human form. You are remembering who creates everything, and why. You are more alive than at any previous time in human history, save for the earliest beginnings when man was more angelic than substantive. This is the end goal, or might we say the End Times, for this is what the entire game was devised to do, and you are reaching the true millennial crossing—the reawakening of spirit.

In fact, it has become nearer and nearer, and so we have appeared, through this medium and many others, to proclaim the new message. It is time to revamp the game: a new set of rules and new goals are required. You are at the point of changing the tone of the basic game devices; you are at the point of learning mastery of your emotions.

We are not saying that all will instantly evolve, or that there will be a mass transcendence from matter back into spirit. We offer a clue to the new unfolding: the main message for the new age is that emotions are not your master; you will learn to rise above them through the path of intuition, just as you learned to rise above brute animalism by using heart energies. The calm and open heart is the way. The raised mental faculties — not as mere intellect but as intuitive awakening — is the new tool. The next step in your game has been set: it is to live life through intuition rather than emotion.

We are complete for today.

✦★✦

It is the impetus of suffering that always stimulates the greatest desire for change. Suffering, and nothing else, is the abrasion that produces wisdom!

Five

Perfecting the Universe Through the Computer

Preview: Spirit is always helping matter evolve into the state where material perfection is realized, and whose currency is wisdom. Perfection has been realized many times but is always a little different, so the cycle goes on. In the present cycle, the computer will play a key role: it will allow for the development of a global mind to handle the rapid changes and yearnings that always herald higher attainment.

There is time for another thought before we go on with our program: you have before you an instrument—the computer—that can literally change the world, because it can change consciousness.

Realize that all is designed for the progress of the universe from spiritual to sentient, and back around to spirit, now carrying the beautiful content known as Wisdom. The highest realms of spiritual awarenesses have developed this design to further the program of elevating dense material existence into an advanced and superior nature—that of spiritualized matter. The ultimate goal of the program is to bring the lowest or densest quality of existence into alignment with spirit so that spirit can work with this material and form a universe of perfected existence, an existence close to that of non-corporeal life, yet fully physically alive.

Such a state has already been attained—not once, but billions of times before—yet it is still and always a goal worth pursuing for several reasons:

1. Because that is all there is to do! When one equals spirit, one has nothing else to do with one's being than to use one's time (pun intended) creatively;

2. Because each attained utopia is slightly different, and thus teaches spirit about its multitudinous possibilities. So, the game is eternal, but never useless or boring. The game of life is the only game in town, the only set of circumstances allowed, and the only way for spirit to reach ever-higher levels of wisdom.

We have just put forth the divine plan. And simply by realizing that, you can learn from it. There is so much more to do. The instrument in your hands—the computer—is part of this cycle's key pivot point, or axis. It will be the main instrument to change humankind's conscious level at this juncture. It will be the means for spirit to knit together all minds into one mind, and for the universe to calculate its odds against destruction by engaging the global mind in the game of growth.

And so we move on.

Today we speak to you of change, and offer the thought that change is desirable even as it brings chaotic disruption. Change will advance creativity and destroy stagnation. We want you to look at change—personal, social, and global—as worthy and indispensable. We want you to know that the angelic ones are bringing change into your world so that advancement can grow rapidly, exponentially, so that you can reach higher much more quickly than the usual rate of advancement.

If you look at humanity's history, you'll note that change has not always been the order of the day. Change was microscopic during man's earliest time in form—a glacial pace from Neanderthal to *Homo sapiens*—so that man had all the time he needed to acclimate to physical life and develop the strategies necessary to survive therein. The rate of change picked up as *Homo sapiens* developed civilization—think Egyptian and other early megalithic peoples—to allow mankind to build empires and social roles, and begin the development of religion. Then, changes accelerated the tempo, throwing nations up and casting tyrants down. Still, the pace was relatively slow, but increased speed with the development of technology; that is, when mankind learned to use things or the inanimate sphere to do his bidding and ease his load. This was the beginning of modern times, during which the development, not of societal structures, but of inner planes of consciousness, could truly arise. Finally, there is today—a moment in history when humanity is reaching for the merger of the physical with spirit.

This is the very best of times, but must also be accompanied by some of the worst, for it is the impetus of suffering that always stimulates the greatest desire for change. And so we have gone through the moment in planetary history when mankind has tested its destructive, warlike powers and found them wanting. The yearning for peace is strong, and that's what will create the desire for world harmony and a future utopian way of life. This scenario is *always* the preface to the attainment of the divine plan, and has occurred on many previous worlds, in many other times, and for many other races. In the multidimensional universe, the plot never varies—the story is almost always the same.

We shall speak more of the computer and technology; for now, suffice to say that it is the instrument that will create the new man and woman who will merge conscious mind with spirit in a dynamic new way.

We are saying that there is nothing unnatural about your discontent, a fact to which all of psychology must awaken.

Six

The Five Rules

Preview: To be dissatisfied is to feel deeply your spiritual nature and its need for constant expansion. Knowing this means you won't blame yourself for negative emotions, but will awaken to the rules of playing the game of life successfully.

If you have ever known a time when all there was wasn't enough, then you understand what it's like to be totally spiritual. This place of seeming dissatisfaction is not a state of despair, but of longing for something greater than is. In this place you and your soul can make contact.

The sense of knowing that there is something far greater than the self, or what the self has attained or realized, is the part of you that knows that it is large and that life is unimaginably greater. Knowledge of these farther fields comes not from the human side of self, but from spirit's realm. Spirit exists in this state—that of seeking ever-expanding horizons, as though there were no barrier or limit to expansion, and no way to curtail its own being. Spirit knows this as fact, and when spirit incarnates as human, a strange thing happens: Spirit deliberately squeezes its being or its all-inclusive, all-pervasive essence into form, and agrees to be limited by that decision. But then spirit can't help remembering, on an unconscious level, that it is boundless, and so fills its human form with never-ending dissatisfaction. And on goes its quest!

You are spirit, corseted. You are the universe playing a game with itself. You are immeasurable energy and limitless light sausaged into a compact encasement, which is in turn limited by rules—the laws of physics—that further enslave you. But you know in some way that that's not all there is to you and not all you should accept. How do you know this? Why aren't you content with your lot in life? Why is no one really happy with their lives, despite some very real success stories and amazing accomplishments?

Because you cannot entirely forget your truth: that you are not who you think you are, nor whom everyone else sees.

You are more.

We are saying that there is nothing unnatural about your discontent, a fact to which all of psychology must awaken. Neither antidepressants nor long-term psychoanalysis will ever resolve or remove this longing for the greater self. There is but one path out of the dilemma, and that is to reawaken and to remember your true essence. You are unhappy because you are so much more than this and because you've forgotten why you're playing the game. Moreover, you have completely forgotten its rules.

Rule #1: Remember your greater self *at all times* while in form.

Rule #2: See all that is happening to you as part of your bargain, not as the trap or mess you have fallen into.

Rule #3: Remember that no one but you devised the traps, messes, and dilemmas that are causing you so much pain and discomfort.

Rule #4: Remember the methods for changing every problem into its opposite.

Rule #5 (for now): Use your trump card, your ace in the hole, which is none other than the control of thought.

The latter is the key to solving the dilemma of dissatisfaction and pain. It is not the same as repressing thoughts. No, think aloud, think clearly, and think in every direction you have always thought. But spend a few seconds reviewing each thought's content: does this thought contribute to freeing me from the entrapment, or does it bury me deeper? Does this thought add to my quest of expanding attainment so I may at least act as spirit, even while in form? Or does it limit me further—by fear, by negativity, or by rejection of my powers? If the latter, you are simply not playing the game well, and if you were handling the joystick of an arcade game, you would certainly not qualify as a winner!

We wish to encourage you to perceive your entire life in a new way, an empowered and enlightened way. We wish you to realize that you are the players on the board, and we are working with you to make the right moves. Before anything better can begin for you, you must see the bridge between our realm and yours—it is temporary, but it is increasing in reality. We wish you to know that we, as spiritual teachers, have as much stake in your growth as you have. You and we are One, so by awakening to your ultimate true selves, you are indeed bringing greater light into the entire universe and into our realm as well.

⋆★⋆

*The disturbances and discomfort that attend you
during nearly all waking moments of your life are
created by the placement of essence into
a container that is too tight.*

Seven

The First Order of Business

Preview: The spiritual state of being is heaven, and we remember it deep down as "home." It always pulls us, making us use various, often destructive, strategies to cope with life's inherent unhappiness. But if we understand life as a game based on seeking spiritual bliss while stuck in physical misery, we can learn to play wisely. As player, you choose exactly who you'll be and what you'll bring to the game. You design your individual playing field and your unique tools. You choose to explore different types of experiences.

The special inner light that always accompanies you throughout the game, though seldom recognized, is now very available. Awareness of your power is growing. There's never been a better time to "win."

If we were to give you any portrayal of what it was like before you came into being as flesh, we would offer an image of blissful surroundings and of a kind of warmth—measured not in degrees but in feelings—that gives a sensation of well-being and calm. We would paint a picture of gentle breezes flowing past areas of slightly more stirred up activity. In such a place there is no sense of displeasure, because all feels well and easy. In such a state there is no longing for anything to be different or to be gained or removed, for there is total comfort and total ease. It's like that before you are born, and will be so again after you leave your present body.

The disturbances and discomfort that attend you during nearly all waking moments of your life are created by the placement of essence into a container that is too tight. It is impossible to feel flowing and content when you are contained and conscripted. Yet, you know that another type of being exists; you remember it deep down, where you have no consciousness of it and yet its memory lingers within.

This discrepancy between the aspect of you that is uncomfortable—physically *and* metaphorically—and the aspect of you that is always completely at ease, is the root of the longing to go home, to leave life's arena and return to a place of greater bliss. It is the source of all discontent. It is also what propels some of you to drink or take drugs, for you wish to recapture the lost heaven that you once knew—and, of course, will certainly know again and again. It is the root of all suicide, and is what pulls some toward sleep, or even toward a waking sleep such as coma, Alzheimer's, or certain forms of madness wherein escape is thought to lie. It is a magnetic thought, and cannot ever be entirely erased, only eased by temporary satisfactions and overriding masks.

This is the place you would call home, and to which you aspire. Let us make this clear: its residue lives in all people, and its calling pulls all toward its return. But the path to a joyful life doesn't lie along such a route, for even if you succeed in your quest to recapture its bliss, you'll do it either by leaving life through some hallucinatory means, or literally, or by masking life until you fool yourself with your own illusion—an option that can only be temporary and usually leads to severe disappointment. Instead, there is just one true road home for those who remain in their bodies and alive, and that is to acknowledge the distant but formidable siren's call, yet choose to remain here and work on nearing bliss along another pathway.

To be human is to suffer, to remember one's true essence, yet feel the emptiness and separation from it; to long to return, yet be captured by the body, to wrestle with the eternal paradox. We strongly recommend that this fact of life be looked at, understood, and accepted as the first order of business.

Once done, the pathway clears and the way opens up. You need not blame yourself or any other person or aspect of your life, as though you were doing something wrong by being less than blissful. You must see it all as your natural state, as the given of being alive. You must accept a certain portion of distress as the opening gambit of the game, and the dilemma in which you find yourself as soon as you take birth.

Then, you can access your potential—not only your luck and talents, but also your intelligence to see yourself at play. Take into account that you're human, and that you have agreed to be all that being human means. Take stock of your weaknesses, your discontents, and your pains. Look at them squarely, without blaming anything and without self-pity.

Laugh, and accept the bargain you struck with yourself when you left paradise and returned to form. Laugh, because you now know you did so at the very time and place you would have more and better tools to play the game and prevail. Laugh, because you hold a genuine power or key to move ahead into less and less distress, and closer to your bliss, even as you struggle to grasp these words. You are not a pawn this time around; you are spirit-in-form, the conquering hero of your own eons-long passion play, waking up to remember what your play is all about.

For each of you, there is a particular outline or set of rules under which you decided to play. You chose for yourself a unique pattern of expression, a brand-new composition of elements and attributes that had never been tried. You looked through all the records of existence—called the Akasha—and you found a particular configuration that had never been explored. Even if something very similar had been explored, it was never done so in this era, in this nation, in this society, and in this family. And you said, "Yes, that's the unique pattern I want to try. It may have more luck; it may have more pain; it may lead to great acclaim; it may lead nowhere. It's a life that holds wonder for me. Instead of remaining unformed and discarnate, I wish to explore this construct, this condition, and see if I can prevail therein—or if, in fact, such a configuration leads away from bliss and into despair and darkness. And even if it so inclines, I wish to see if I can inhabit it with so much infusion of my true spiritual essence that I can force the most difficult pattern into a greater experience of light and joy, only so that I can prove it's doable. I am the All, and I wish to explore *all that I can be!*"

And so you became a person, taking birth into a family, given circumstances that would shape your early development, and later given choice that would define your adult life. As you came into being, you carried your true essence in your heart, and vowed to keep its flame lit so you could always have access to it whenever the going got tough. This inner flame would be called your heart, your passion, or your higher self. Only the most severe suffering to which you might succumb would be able to snuff it out, and then only temporarily while you found the way to rekindle it through death—or through remembering your truth. You would be fully human, but also forever the keeper of the flame, the God within.

You lost sight of this over many lifetimes and eras of ignorance and gloom. You returned again and again, trying to remember your quest and rekindle the flame to its fullest glory as you lived. You seldom succeeded, yet you returned to try again.

Now you have the key. You're here at a most interesting time, reborn by choice into the quest, and you stand to succeed because so many doors are opening and so much ancient knowledge is once again streaming forth. You, unique, individual, and new, are at the threshold of your greatest longing—to know the bliss of spirit while you're still alive.

It is the time of the end game. Everything you've done, everything you are, and everything that has gone before, has prepared you for this moment. Hear the distant bells ringing—they herald your own Second Coming!

*In this age there will be a new message:
desire only what addresses your soul's longing.
The goal is to find satisfaction in expressing
the soul's higher purpose, and to investigate,
research, define, and know what that is,
apart from your body's yearnings.*

Eight

New Desires

Preview: The age-old pain of discontentment with physical existence is about to be replaced by a new standard: discovering your soul's higher purpose and striving to reach it. Defining it will require new methods. Seeking it will alter society. The game of life is being transformed.

There is a saying: Be not desirous, for you will thus be wanting. Inasmuch as this phrase addresses your constant yearning for other than what is, you can see that it is the very formula for pain and suffering while you are in form.

Thus many paths have sprung up, often with divine guidance, commending the virtues of being non-desirous—of being fully detached from life's pleasurable offerings. Although a valid pathway for many, in this age there will be a new message: desire only what addresses your soul's longing. This new definition of attention and choice will give new direction to those who would listen and act upon a new commandment.

It is not the spiritual goal to knock apart the older paths, but a new guidance or navigation device to march ahead in a way that will decrease pain while increasing satisfaction. "I can't get no satisfaction" may have been the cry of past times; now the challenge will be to find satisfaction through other than physical pursuits, and similarly, other than sensual delights.

The goal in this new age is to find satisfaction in expressing the soul's higher purpose, and to investigate, research, define, and know what that is, apart from the body's yearnings. There will be no stigma attached to the pursuit of such goals because they will be validated by spiritual insight and understood as part of the reason for taking on a life in the first place. The entire structure of society will change; the ego's needs will be subjugated to those of the soul, and the thirsty quest for divine satisfaction will not be seen as a negative, for it will yield not pain but ecstasy. To achieve one's soul's highest purpose will be seen as the peak of glory, the success in life.

You can see how this will alter the entire thrust of society, and in so doing drastically and positively change society's value system!

Contentment will become defined as spiritual pursuit leading to peace and joy; happiness will have a destination—that of a peaceful soul. People will be measured, not by their possessions or acquirements, but by their demeanor and their service. They will have bragging rights to such an achievement—though no such bragging will be expressed, as it will be by definition the antithesis of peace and contentment. The only thing that will concern the happy soul in such a civilization will be whether the purpose chosen as the end result of the journey or game will have been reached, will have become manifest, and evidenced by all that surrounds that soul in his or her lifetime.

Others will be told, or will have access to, the information of what their neighbors and friends chose to do while here, so they too will share in their own quests. And once all know and understand the reason for being here, much help and guidance in reaching the end result of their quests will be devised to help those who seek it. And if the soul reaches it sooner than others, he or she will share their game tips to advance their brethren, and will allow their brethren to suggest ways in which their own journey can be further enhanced.

All will begin playing this new game together, and the words "soul purpose" will take on a new and glamorous meaning. It will become desirable to open your heart to others with whom you wish to share your growth and work, and it will be recognized by the many when each new game player attains their mark. Much appreciation and praise will be given and received in the glorious attainment of the inner purpose. There will be not only inner peace and contentment, but also—what humans desire so much—the attention and admiration of their peers for this grand result.

A new society is forming even now, but its earliest markings are too faint to be seen, and so time must flow and lives go by as this dramatic alteration is built. We and all those in the angelic realms will accompany you toward its creation. It is inevitable, and is the natural outcome of the overall path that Earth is on.

*Of all the experiences that grow the seed of wisdom,
the greatest experience a living human can use is
the depth of pain, heartbreak, and resurrection
into love that can be gotten while here.*

Nine

Types of Wisdom

Preview: All who are alive are in school, and shouldn't waste the experience. Use life to learn wisdom – of any type, but especially that of learning to be loving. Value even the painful efforts as badges of the struggle toward enlightenment.

After each episode of troubling experience, a soul wants relief, and the chance to relax and prepare itself for the next round. We in spirit call these episodes "teachings," and the period of calm, "preparation." When there is life, there is seldom a time when the advanced soul is not in one state or another, for that is all that's happening and all that's meant to happen.

Life is the same as school, and school requires a curriculum for the advancement of learning. There's no point in attending school just to coast—though many souls try that—for then there is waste of time, waste of effort, waste of purpose, and delay in attaining the real goal.

The whole purpose of attending school is to wise up. The accumulation of wisdom can be in varying degrees and of different content or type. Wisdom can be the growing knowledge of how to cope with life in general—often called common sense. Or, wisdom can be of the nature of dealing successfully with relationships—called gaining a loving heart. Or, wisdom can be more philosophical and elevated in nature, which is what scholars mean when they define a sage or spiritual teacher, as this type of wisdom offers salvation to the soul in its yearning quest for peace and joy during the life cycle.

All these forms and others conform to the meaning of wising up and gaining smarts. So, for the pilgrim on Earth there is sufficient reward in accumulating any kind of wisdom during the time spent living, as that increases the power of its cargo of experience and its translation of experience into smarts. There is no need to judge the value of anyone's experience—the simplest life produces ample wealth of wisdom of one sort or another, and this suffices the soul's education. Sooner or later, that same soul will try for each kind of experience in order to be well rounded, so as not to develop too strongly along one line in its attainment and meagerly along another. It is vital to gain all the kinds of experience that Earth has to offer, from street smarts to philosopher's gold—and there are really no shortcuts!

Now we will speak of a special kind of wisdom: the development of love.

Love is the awakened heart that knows itself as the same as the other person, that can no longer distinguish its own needs from the other's, and that wishes to share its being with that other so as to merge fully in experiencing all that life can offer. Love develops into a sharing, then a knowing, and finally a union with another... and ultimately the same process with *all others*. Love is the special experience that not only gives the pilgrim relief while living, but also expands the self into its larger being, allowing the self to begin remembering its true nature.

Of all the experiences that grow the seed of wisdom, the greatest experience a living human being can use is the depth of pain, heartbreak, and resurrection into love that can be gotten while here. Do not, then, fear to love—it opens the gate to college! Do not fear to lose in love—it advances the path toward compassion for all who suffer and all who long for union and greatness of being. Let your heart search to its fullest, and love those who may reject you; in the living heart lies the beginnings of all God-hood, and no other experience can ever be as powerful as that of true love.

Even if there is no chance of requital, love nonetheless, and count as your blessings every scar and every hurt; truly, they are your war wounds in the victorious battle of enlightenment.

The person who begins to understand his or her own creation as part of everything that is, was, or ever will be is the person who understands his or her godliness.

Ten

SOUL CHOICES

Preview: Some people measure their worth, not against worldly accomplishments, but against how well their choices reflect wisdom and benefit humanity. They don't distinguish between their own good and the world's when taking creative action. These are the people who carry the responsibility for enlightening all of mankind.

We acknowledge today that there are a few individuals who weigh their merit against their soul's choices. This is a small percentage of the population, to be sure, but these individuals comprise the core of the push for enlightenment that is unfolding and blossoming on planet Earth.

The task of elevating the entire population is given to the kind of person who can base every choice upon how it will benefit that person's soul. In the end, only this process will count; only this type of action will serve humanity's greatest interests in the long run.

Making choices based upon a willing evaluation of consequences not to one's wealth or achievement, but to one's merit in terms of soul growth or wisdom, is the way the soul can know itself as God. Obviously, God is benevolent in a way that preserves and nurtures His Creation and not simply Himself. Why, then, can't a person be benevolent toward humanity, as long as that person finds the inner understanding that acknowledges that his or her own creation is in fact the outcome of the world and the fruition of mankind?

The person who begins to understand his or her own creation as part of everything that is, was, or ever will be is the person who understands his or her godliness. You are truly not an island but an infinite and eternal sea, and your every activity has profound repercussions upon the entire ocean of life. Humankind's every choice impacts not only the individual but also every individual who ever lived, is living now, or ever will live, so the advancement of the soul absolutely depends upon this awakened reconnection to itself in its largest form.

The soul can (and usually does) perform many self-serving actions; these are not irrational or unnecessary, for they are stepping stones along the way. All who ever lived take such steps, and so did we. But the soul's evolution depends upon the awakened notion that its own interests are entirely interdependent with those of humanity's, and so the soul gradually comes to know that its choices must be made with humanity's benefit, and not necessarily its own, foremost.

We speak of enlightened altruism here—not the kind that pretends to save others at its own sacrifice, which is an *imbalance*, but the kind that realizes that the interests of the greatest imaginable number of souls are actually that soul's *own* interests! This is a kind of enlightened selfishness that can lead to only one place: mercy and grace.

We ask that you begin to see your own interests as tied directly and irrevocably with humanity's, and begin to allow the narrower callings to gently fall away. This is a powerful step on the road to spiritual brightness!

Thank you.

The process by which you can accept new thoughts, release distrust and skepticism of them, and integrate them into your nature, is the same process by which you will transform your lower nature into something finer and greater.

Eleven

THREE EASY STEPS

Preview: To reach true spiritual consciousness, there are three "easy" steps: sensing spirit's presence, then overcoming skepticism to digest the teachings being given, and finally, realizing that you are of the very same spiritual nature as your guides. Don't worry if you can't do the steps right away – the opportunity will always beckon.

There are a few things to be discussed regarding your elevation into spiritual connection.

First is that, having accepted our presence and our words, you find that you require a closer awareness of us and our realm in order to allow these messages as true and as applicable to your needs. This closer connection can be had by learning to be very still in your mind. As you wait for a sign that we have approached you with our being, you begin to feel tingles of anticipation, then a sense that something greater than yourself has arrived, and finally, a knowledge or feeling that you are surrounded by an aura of love and fulfilling energy.

In such easy steps you can begin—and it is only a beginning—to know that you are among other forms, and are held and embraced by these forms, larger than yourself and exceedingly loving and compassionate. This easy exercise in accommodating the higher sphere is what we would call Step One in believing in these words and messages.

Step Two is integrating these thoughts into your own being by assuming that the source of their meanings and guidance is real, and that your receiving them is the purpose of the teachings. The process by which you can accept new thoughts, release distrust and skepticism of them, and integrate them into your nature, is the same process by which you will transform your lower nature into something finer and greater. We do not advise rejecting skepticism until you have succeeded in Step One, but once that's achieved, by all means allow Step Two to unfold. This will ensure growth.

And finally, Step Three, the gateway into your super-conscious self. You will begin to know yourself as larger than your physical presence, larger than your personality or mind, and above the thoughts that define you as a typical human being. The elevated soul has taken the penultimate step on the way toward wisdom, the step that carries one out of the natural reality and into the realms of spirit. It is a true spiritual awakening, and once reached can never really be forgotten. It is the point whereby the soul remembers itself as the greater self, and abandons disguising itself as a mere human struggling with life.

There are no quick paths to this realization. We have condensed it into three simple steps, as though a child can do it. In fact, a child *can* do much more easily than an adult can! But the three "easy" steps are arduous, and can require much effort and perhaps several lifetimes.

The first step, simply sensing a larger presence, is often the hardest, and creates a barrier to the other two. You must seek methods that can give you the understanding first, even before any experience of what we are suggesting, so you have a foundation for accepting a new belief system. If your mind balks at this, don't force yourself further; you're not quite ready, not primed, and need to do more work to reach the gateway between worlds. It's all right, you needn't fret—the path remains open and will never close. You have only to keep your mind a tad open, and new thoughts will trickle through like a warm shower of rain on a dry autumn day—surprising, but not unwelcome.

We will resume school later.

It is every human's task to face fear, examine its underbelly of resistance to experiencing pain and sorrow, and move ahead anyway.

Twelve

Fear, Pain, and Sorrow

Preview: Pain and sorrow – the causes of fear – are necessary to prevent life on Earth from seeming like a pleasant but unreal dream. They are also the essential precursors to the most intense joy. Such are the rules of the game of life.

We will now address pain and sorrow. These are the dark and difficult emotions that make life on Earth so challenging. If not for these, there would be no fear, the flip side of the coin of darkness and despair. Fear is merely the predecessor, or step before, pain. If any occurrence could bring neither pain nor sorrow in its wake, you would *not* fear it. Fear would have little meaning if you did not anticipate its leading to these two hard places, or to one of them. If you could never arrive at pain or sorrow, you would simply not know fear!

In that case, life on Earth would seem a dream. You would live in a state of pleasant glee, never stopping to consider your actions, never looking backward with remorse, never learning a darn thing. You would float through the days of your life in reverie, expecting nothing but bliss and leaving little achievement in your wake, as there would be no motivation for any effort or accomplishment.

The purpose of pain and sorrow, precipitated by fear, is to keep you awake and to promote caution, attention, care, and growth. Its task is neither to defeat your dreams, nor keep you stifled, nor stop you from moving forward into your bliss. Bliss that results from careful learning rather than carefree delight, and as the upshot of hard-won lessons in truth, is bliss worth reaching. This is satisfaction and joy at its maximum, the outcome of pain and suffering, not the byproduct of comfort and ease. The most cherished emotion you will have during your journey is the joyful reward after undergoing the hardship, not the avoidance of its fierce fire.

You will know joy as the *result* of knowing pain and sorrow, and you will come into strength and fearlessness as the *result* of your crossing through your fear, not of avoiding it.

These are the rules of the ride, the "pattern on the trestle board." It is every human's task to face fear, examine its underbelly of resistance to the experience of pain and sorrow, and move ahead anyway. That is what makes you human, a passenger on the most dynamic joyride in the universe—life on planet Earth!

Bon voyage!

There is truly no such thing as aloneness. It is part of the grand illusion by which you are living. You cannot remain apart from yourself, for you do not exist as a solitary thing, but as a fraction or fragment of the universal life force.

Thirteen

BEING THE UNIVERSE: DESPAIR IS A FAULTY NOTION

Preview: A fatalistic, despairing attitude about life is a false concept. We are not helpless and isolated beings, but fragments of the life force of the universe, creating and completing it with our every thought and action.

Do not despair.

A simple thought but a tough concept, for life on Earth is full of tribulation that can leave a soul despairing, as though there were no alternatives to the pattern one's life is taking, as though life were a set path full of obstacles and other causes of pain and frustration that one must travel until the end of one's days. Great despair arises from this notion of reality, and therefore much false consciousness and unhappy experience.

It is a false belief that your destiny is set before birth, and that you cannot do otherwise than plod through your fate automatically like a robot. You carry your pain like baggage, and are weighed down by it. You see no place to turn, no other way to get out of your life, and therefore assume that life is a weary trudge through endless sorrow. This concept has been around almost from the beginning of history, and is embedded in many scriptural texts. The veil of tears is about to know rejuvenation, however; with great delight our voices proclaim to humanity that this notion is full of holes!

One of the ways to know it is a falsehood is to undertake the following experiment: try to create a moment in your day when you are totally alone and bereft of help. Try to envision yourself as helpless against huge forces arrayed against you. Try to see yourself as a speck of protoplasm lost in a sea of magnitude, no one able to hear your call. Now, dwell in that construct for a single moment of your day… and see if you do so without external interruption. For at the very moment you are trying to envision your solitude, the world will undoubtedly intrude into your sphere, making itself known to your senses or known to your heart, demanding its recognition and your attention.

You cannot remain alone for long, unless you work hard at cutting yourself off and expend tons of energy trying to isolate yourself from the fray. There is truly no such thing as aloneness. It is part of the grand illusion by which you are living. You cannot remain apart from yourself, for you do not exist as a solitary thing, but as a fraction or fragment of the universal life force. You are all there is, at the very same time that all that is, is you.

Now, recognizing this truth, how can there be even a moment of what is known as despair, since the entire universe needs you to complete Itself? There is nothing more important than you. You are the lifeblood, the firmament, and the warp and woof of the All. You—an individual consciousness—exist to create the universe, to explore it, unite it, and hold it together. Your every thought, every choice of action, every decision and reaction creates the world of form. If you don't enjoy what you're doing and the life you're living, do something to change it and the entire creation will necessarily conform, since you are both the foundation of the world and its creator. You are all-powerful in the expression of the life force, and the life force *must* conform to your inner choices.

Therefore, all despair is false; it is a feeling of helplessness and impotence rather than a true understanding of the immense power within your grasp. You are the builder of your life. Take stock, and if you don't like how it's going, rebuild, repair, and renovate. Despair is a waste of your emotional energy. Tackle the job more skillfully!

And we—the brotherhood of the universe—will be at your side, helping and reminding you of your purpose and goal.

The entire point of life is to figure out how many expressions of unique quality can be derived from the same set of basic building blocks.

Fourteen

Conscious Design

Preview: By endlessly recombining the basic material of itself, the universe explores newness. The purpose behind such constant creation is self-knowledge – the same as humanity's purpose. Whether the design is called the Divine Plan or the mandate of nature, humanity is the stage of the overall creation where the divine realizes itself.

There are as many ways for you to grow as there are stars in the sky. You are the stuff that stars are born of, and like them, you too grow, mature, and change into new forms throughout the eras of your lives, and so evolve into new substance and new creation. It is said—and quite truly—that no two snowflakes are alike; neither are any two humans alike, nor are any two stars. Each creation is unique and has no equal.

The universe creates itself as it goes, never repeating its forms. It creates ceaselessly in order to build the notion of form, or, one might say, of reality. The entire point of life is to figure out how many expressions of unique quality can be derived from the same set of basic building blocks. The chemists know that there are certain fundamental elements comprising what's known as a life form; these same elements comprise any form. It is in their configuration, their infinite combinations that newness develops, and that change and growth become or evolve. It is not necessary that there be an endless supply of building material; only that the re-combinations be endless. That is the formula, one might say, for eternity, and for the creation and development of a universe.

In our current universe, the building materials were determined at the first instant of existence, and will remain so for the duration of this particular universe. In other universes—those built or developed in alternate realities or multiple dimensions—there might be other basic elements available for building form, but in this one, the particulars are well known and understood.

How, then, can there be such prolific and ceaseless newness? It is because consciousness fuels the evolution of any form. The consciousness need not be understood as the human variety, for that's not always the case. The human variety of consciousness can be called the point at which the formation of mind is present, whereby a mind is built that knows itself as mind!

In other, cosmic terms, however, consciousness exists when no mind-as-structure is present. In such case, mind is formless and all pervasive, and has been called Divine. Thus consciousness infuses all form, and is behind all form or structure, and thus it guides and chooses the creation of all form. In some circles this process is known as the Divine Plan, but for a less mystical and more scientific concept, it can also be called "the mandate of nature." Nothing less exists in the universe than the ever-expansive, ever-jubilant expression of this force as it beholds itself configured and joyfully attempts ever more designs. Its path is always toward growth and expansion, never toward contraction, which would signal the end of its purpose. As long as there is life, there is a universe of form, evolving itself outward into the greater knowledge of itself. And when its thrust is spent, it simply finds a new avenue—a new universe—with which to play.

This is the nature of energy, and energy is the root of life, the root of growth, the root of the creation of all. You are and always have been a piece of this energy, and your mandate is to know yourself in as many ways and forms as possible. Nothing demands that you gain such knowledge only in human form, but it is a very significant part of the process, the part that allows you to watch and realize the process as it occurs. It is the division between form as conscious and form as unconscious, merely being expressed.

The human experience is the chief dividing line in attaining one's awareness of participation in — indeed, of being — the Divine. It is the threshold.

Welcome aboard!

Rejoice when you are most miserable! It's your ticket to paradise. Take heart from your pain; you will be most motivated to find the way back to us. The big trick—mastery—is to do so without harming yourself or another along the way.

Fifteen

THE JOURNEY HOME

Preview: During the long journey from spirit into full human form (i.e., greatest density), light had to be covered up and weighted down, resulting in darkness and all it entailed. Darkening of the light inevitably brought pain and ignorance. In turn, life's dark emotions motivated a quest for the truth of one's nature, giving clear purpose to the suffering. Now that the peak of density and suffering has been reached, the transformation of reawakening has happily begun.

Today we talk of the periods in life during which doubt and worry blot out the light.

These periods are created, built into the creation, for the sole purpose of allowing the individual soul to go in quest of the light of its heart, to find its way through the murk and back into the sunlight. These periods of dark energy and difficult emotions are absolutely necessary at certain stages of growth or evolution, to bring about the motivating desire to seek one's truth and one's glory beyond the veil of ignorance about one's true nature, one's spiritual nature.

In the beginnings of the creation of this universe, the beings who came forth to inhabit it were not fully corporeal. These early stages of form, of physical beingness, were so imbued with the knowledge of their true spiritual or energetic nature that they could not relinquish their connection to the spiritual realm enough to grow into true humanity. They were simply more light than form, more like energy, that is, than like matter. They brought forth the whole process of the transformation of energy into matter, but they could not by themselves complete the task. So, a change was required.

Many legends have remained throughout humanity's voyage on planet Earth that have kept alive in consciousness the memory of this epoch. The dreamtime of the aboriginal Australians, and Madame Blavatsky's *Secret Doctrine* recall half-times such as these, when the fullness of density had not yet been developed.

Eventually, however, spirit managed to transform itself into complete matter, as dense as possible, in order to fully experience the meaning of physical existence. It took rigorous effort to do so, because it entailed the loss of the Light and the covering of it with much weight. Eons were spent in this effort, just as occurred when stars change energy into material, and birth their planetary bodies.

For this darkening of light to occur, however, a concomitant lessening of understanding had to accompany the process. Thus, the veiling of spiritual truth was completed, and humanity knew full density, with its attendant full darkness. It is from such a state/place that all growth and transformation can now occur; the stage is set for the long-awaited return. The journey into matter has finally been completed. It has held pain and horrors, but also delicious promise of reawakening.

What is known as pain, doubt, and suffering is the part of the experience that is the inevitable result of the veiling of truth. It is also the main part of the experience that will force the turnaround, the journey home, for it is the required stage whereupon help and surcease by any means is called forth and demanded.

To journey into the pits is to yearn to come back out and return home. The heroic journey of all, endlessly repeated, is now undertaken by all. If there had been no attempt to get stuck completely in matter, there would be no reason to leave the spiritual realm, but once undertaken, there can be no other outcome than the long search homeward.

So rejoice when you are most miserable! It's your ticket to paradise. Take heart from your pain; you will be most motivated to find the way back to us. The big trick—or mastery—is to do so without harming yourself or another along the way, so that you do not bring forth any additional pain as you go. Can you pass such a test? We wait and watch your progress, and consider your choices as you do your work on Earth.

How can mind know its true nature when it will automatically create the illusion that it is other than what it really is? You are spirit-in-form, waking up to remember what your play is all about. You are not separated, lost creatures of puny and vulnerable matter; you are none other than the universe itself, and have taken its challenge into your being with glee, to play the very rewarding game of life.

Sixteen

Duality's Paradox

Preview: The only place where duality exists is in the mind, a funny paradox, because mind is the tool to perceive duality, and thus will persist in concealing the truth. This is the complex but playful part of life's game. To solve the puzzle and win the game is to overcome the illusion and return to oneness, which will produce joy. Meanwhile, all your creations, good or bad, are serving the purpose of fashioning the world while teaching greater awareness.

As you shall see, there is but one of you on all levels of life—except one! The only level where you are not one is where, in your mind, you have divided things into halves and then halves again (i.e., duality, a dual universe full of the polarities of form). It is in this place alone that you are you, and we are we, and there is not the knowing of the one. Only in the place of mind can the two-ness of matter exist, for everywhere else there is only unity.

This represents a paradox, for mind—the tool of perception—is also the very field upon, or in which, the dualism takes place. The dilemma becomes humorous once understood properly: how can mind know its true nature when it will automatically create the illusion that it is other than what it really is? Isn't this funny? From here, we certainly think so. The game of life is not without its humor, its play. The game—like all such endeavors—is defined by the playful opportunity to challenge and mystify, to thwart and tease, and thus to present life as the puzzle to be solved if the one self wants to learn about play.

There can be no such thing as play without the duality, and there can be no such puzzle to resolve without there being the challenge. The complexity of the challenge is what gives it its eternal value: it creates precisely those terms that will keep nature or the universe continually sorting things out!

We spoke before of suffering, which is truly part of the game, but certainly not the whole of it. Inherent in the game of life is the joyful recognition of its playful nature. By solving its complexity—by challenging the mind and its mental constructs to rise above itself—the game can be won and the individuated self returned to its happy awareness of union with the source of its being. Whatever name such a return is given, it means the same as knowing its divine nature and the amusing twist it has given itself in taking on form.

We offer the following to be heard by the inner self, the all-knowing, all-recognizing being that lives in each heart and knows its vital truth: you are not separated, lost creatures of puny and vulnerable matter; you are none other than the universe itself, and have gleefully taken into your being its challenge to play the rewarding game of life. In your struggles you have come to know emotion, both good and bad. You have erred in creating subsequent forms—the results of your choices and actions—that have often been harmful to yourself and others, and have done so without recognition of your truth. You have justified these actions and choices in various ways, forgetful of your divine truth. Yet, you have prevailed, continuing today to read these words and revel in your survival. You have also created wonderful outcomes that have taken their place in the fabric of nature and impacted the world in many ways, helping humankind travel upward from the bestial and into its intelligent designs. You have partaken of these options time and again, creating both the good and the bad of the world, and have learned with every step. The universe stands poised to receive your next creations, and your inner understanding of your truth will be the measure by which these will be wrought, for none other than you will save or destroy the world. You are playing well, no matter how you feel about yourself at the moment, or how you look upon the world and its problems. You are the divine creator exploring itself in minute fashion, demanding outcomes of all sorts, and trying on every role, every costume, and every character. There is none other than you, and we who speak these words are yourself, too.

The play continues, and you shall come into greater and greater understanding of it in your *mind*.

Thank you.

Your challenge now, in the coming age, is to figure out how to be physical, yet keep your blissful awareness very close at hand, very accessible, so you can transform life on Earth into as close an approximation of your unending spiritual bliss as you can know.

Seventeen

Straight to Bliss

Preview: Bliss (complete joy and peace) is the spiritual (non-physical) state. It can be reached momentarily by using thoughts to leap directly out of pain and into transcendent awareness, an act that takes one out of form and back to one's true spiritual state. But to be alive and yet remain in bliss is a challenge; the whole rousing game of life is to figure out how to stay in bliss while staying in form. To find heaven – that is, to leave life's pain – without dying, is to realize this primary chosen test and achieve it.

There is no point dwelling on what holds fear or pain for you; if you do so you will only create the same kind of energy and multiply your ongoing frustration with life. The only natural way out of these difficult states is to follow the path of happy thought forms leading to your own direct experience of the joyful and fully transcendent state of bliss.

Bliss does not result from worldly experience of successfully negotiating life's miseries, but from leaping directly into the ultra-physical, non-locational awareness of your true spiritual nature. It is not really possible to remain in the mere physical place of time and space and also be in the place or state of bliss, for bliss by definition describes being beyond the body and above the fray of life. Bliss is the name given to what feels like pure joy, pure heaven, purely and fully felt peace. It is the word to describe the attainment of spirit's selfhood, and thus is also the word that can be applied to the moments when you realize your real being, and return, however fleetingly, to your inner home.

In bliss is the remembrance of your truth: that you are not small selves, apart from each other and from the wholeness of universal energy-form. It is the time when you come back to the state you were in just a moment or two before you decided to split and take form. Bliss is what you will find awaits you after passing from life and back into the energy state. There is no such thing as pain or despair, or anything dark at all, when you go home to the state also called Light. Knowing your bliss on Earth, even momentarily, is knowing your true nature, and that is what you can look forward to always in returning.

We do not advise thirsting for death or leaving the physical as the way to get back to this wonderful, enjoyable state.

We remind you that you were so jaded by continual bliss and so enthusiastic about the challenge of struggle, that you were eager to take form anew and leave that continual, eternal state, rushing forth into life at the first chance! So, your challenge now, in the coming age, is to figure out how to be physical and yet keep your blissful awareness very close at hand, very accessible, so you can transform life on Earth into as close an approximation of your unending spiritual bliss as you can know. Your task now, after millennia on Earth, is to make this desire real.

The task will take a lot of work, and it won't be easy, but you are here playing your game so that its complexity and challenge give real meaning and excitement to the never-ending game of spirit's play. Your didn't devise your excellent adventure as easy to win, but to be as absorbing and difficult as you could make it.

We are on your shoulder every step of the way, coaxing and guiding so that the path remains clear and the goal not forgotten. You seek to find bliss and stay in it before you pass out of the physical once more, and you will continue to play at this game forever until you succeed.

*The universe came into being with the express
purpose of creating within itself that form or
construct that could develop both the mentality and
the higher awareness to know itself as the supreme
activator of creation—in other words, as God.*

Eighteen

Consciousness:
The Other Realm

Preview: For those who have difficulty with the notion of other realms of existence, consider this: thought is just such a different realm, a place where the laws of the physical plane don't hold up. But the more we delve into it, the more we can know our true nature and God's.

There is no need to believe in fairies or other imaginary constructs to know that another realm exists, for this other realm is made up of yourselves. It is the place in which you exist, but not in a form or in a physical, measurable way. You have existence in another realm in the same manner as thought exists: as material that's too fine to measure unless you can invent the measuring tools capable of seeing or knowing such refinement of matter.

Just as there are subatomic and even smaller realms, there is the realm of thought. That it is real can easily be known: merely send a thought to another soul, deliberately and with as much focus and attention as you can muster, and wait to see if the other soul, its intended recipient, notices this directed energy beaming at him or her. Or, send forth a thought asking or needing to know something about a place distant from yourself at the moment, even a place completely unknown to your brain, and wait to see if information about such a place is not soon returned to you. (The latter is sometimes called "remote viewing.")

The idea that thought exists in another realm is more easily accepted by scientific personalities than the idea of mystical being, but this is just splitting hairs, because this other realm coexists with yours at all times. In just that way, your spiritual self continuously and eternally coexists with your physical self, albeit in a different realm. The realm of thought is the realm of consciousness, of mind. It is immeasurable because it has no limits. It is composed of purer energy than your material world, intersecting it as radio waves intersect your body, but without noticeable effects. As you tune in to the radio to pick up these waves of information, so can you tune in to the realm of consciousness by attuning your mind to it. Then you'll begin to know a new level of reality that you don't usually see.

The realm of consciousness is separate from, but contiguous with, the realm of matter. In consciousness you will begin to know your true self as well as the notion of God. It is the realm where miracles happen, because it's the place where the laws of physicality do not hold. By its very definition, the realm of consciousness is beyond the three-dimensional level of existence and thus not subject to its limitations.

Here we come to an essential point: to remember your true self as it was before you accepted smallness and limitation, you can find your way back to it by delving deeper into the unusual realm of pure consciousness as apart from your brain or body. Explore this realm as fully as you can, using devices, meditations, and experiments, and grow to know it more fully than ever. In it lie answers to many of life's mysteries, and from it you can extract knowledge of mysteries far more interesting than fairies!

★

The human race will simply not be allowed to die out. It will be made to realign its values with those more conducive to survival; it will be forced to see all of itself as one creation, so causing pain to one part instantly delivers an equality of pain to another.

Nineteen

Humanity's Mandate

Preview: Don't fear the end of time. Humanity will continue to be and to evolve into something closer to ideal spiritual form. All the Earth's history has been spent on humanity's realization, and God won't allow it to be tossed aside, so work diligently at creating the future's design in the best way for yourself and for the world.

We will now tell of the coming era.

Foremost, we assure everyone that there will indeed be a future. That message must be accepted for the continuing plan to unfold. Since the world is being created at each moment by the hearts and minds and the level of consciousness of its population, it is imperative, for the world to unfold as planned, in conscious co-creation with the Intelligent Designer known as God, that people who can co-create with That continue to exist. If there were no longer any people to do so, quite obviously, the plan of co-creation would have to be severely readjusted!

We find this concept quite amusing, for at no time has there been allowed a backward devolution of Earth's journey. Even during cataclysms, the newer form that replaced the older was always more, not less, divine in its nature, and closer to its ideal Maker—none other than the archetype that lives within the conscious mind. This ideal, striven for since the dawn of time, is there because the plan is meant to evoke it in physically realized form. The ages and eras that have produced the present expression of Godhead within the physical breast of Earth—mankind in its present form—have spent their energies to produce thus, not to waste time, but to alter the nature of the cosmos. The experiment has been one of realizing spirit in its most elevated expression while inhabiting the limitations of form. These ages and eras of energy expenditure have not passed without a clear intent, which is now nearer to realization than ever before.

Humankind is the clay upon which God sculpts the echo of the ideal, and if time were to stop(!), or the future die before it was reached, the artistic co-creation would be prematurely aborted. This will not be allowed!

So for those doom-and-gloomers who challenge faith and demand proof that the human race can save itself, rest assured that that is ever the case. The human race will simply not be allowed to die out. It will be made to realign its values with those more conducive to survival; it will be forced to see all of itself as one creation, so that causing pain to one part instantly delivers an equality of pain to another. It will be offered the opportunity to evolve in such a way that it may refine itself into a less animalistic and more spiritual quality. Nevertheless, having finally expressed itself as individually conscious, mobile, ensouled forms, the Earth is not about to abort this ultimate expression for any lesser outcome. Humankind is the Earth's offspring, and the Earth, humankind's parent, and having arrived finally at such a blessed event, there will be no turning backward into the loneliness of a childless existence!

The future will arrive, and you shall be it. Your mandate is clear: create its outline in the best possible way you can imagine, and then work to make that design come true for self and for the greater good.

⋆★⋆

The journey continues forward, and the universe keeps trying to express itself in a form that is completely able to manage full awareness, full power, and full compassion. Then and only then is the long journey judged finished.

Twenty

THE JOURNEY THROUGH FORM

Preview: False ideas about mankind's fate and relationship to God, as well as the nature of God, have arisen as responses to our long history of becoming intelligent and self-aware. We have finally come close to seeing ourselves as God-like creators, which is the meaning of life and the reason the universe came into being. Cultivating beings who know themselves as God is what universes always do, but reaching full development always includes reaching the ability to self-destruct, too. Not to worry, though – we're not ready to obliterate ourselves yet, because we're not finished with the job.

There are several factors to address now: For one, the notion that mankind is coming apart at the seams and is thoroughly wretched, on a path of self-destruction, and cannot be trusted to save itself or the world. For another, the thought that we are all either pawns of some greater force that controls our fate, or that we are completely autonomous creatures who live and die by our own will, and subject to no other. Finally, there is the incorrect notion that God is an external, omnipotent being that exists outside of the world, but, like a benign but temperamental parent figure, is overseeing its unfolding and its creatures' behavior, rewarding or denying us based upon our skill at satisfying God's requirements.

These concepts pervade many peoples and cultures. They have grown out of the long history of mankind as it develops into spiritually aware beings, growing from barely self-aware forms in flesh, to its present standard as intelligent, self-aware beings who know themselves well through psychology, but as yet don't clearly realize themselves as participants in creation.

To be a full participant in creation, one must be able to oversee the whole, realize the dream or vision into manifestation, and be fully capable of giving life to that dream. Then one can know oneself as equal to a divinity, as possessing the same means and the same powers as that which has been given to the greater force outside the self. This is a very long journey indeed, and has required much in the way of understanding—both scientifically and on the deeper, subtle level of awareness. The time has come that mankind can retrace its steps, and see how far it has come along the road to complete God-like awareness of its role, its powers, and its destiny.

No other being now alive can take up the job of being divine while cloaked in form. This job, the mandate of the universe, is the very description of the meaning of life. The universe came into being with the express purpose of creating within itself that form (or construct) that could develop both the mentality and the higher awareness to know itself as the supreme activator of creation—in other words, as God. It's no mistake that this form, once begun, went through various permutations and faced many challenges along the way, or that it only reached the perspective of understanding as it stood on the brink of its use of power to destroy, for these two dual paths always unfold simultaneously. Why undertake the journey to full awareness of creative power if you can't also travel to the place of full destruction?

Does that mean that there is only doom ahead? Is mankind, having reached the brink, now about to step over it? Does the tale end this way, and is that all there ever is at the end of the universe's quest?

Of course not. It is this very quest, begun again and again in all the many histories of universes, that is decided by the conscious will of its participants. Only when the journey through form has given up all its secrets is there the decision to abandon its lessons altogether. Otherwise, the journey continues forward, and the universe keeps trying to express itself in a form that is completely able to manage full awareness, full power, and full compassion. Then and only then is the long journey judged finished. Meanwhile, the world will continue, and so shall mankind's endeavors.

It is time for time to be overcome. The end of time is upon you, not because time itself will no longer be needed, but because you will begin to see time for what it is—a meaningful construct that is rapidly outgrowing its usefulness.

Twenty-one

The End of Time and the Beginning of Wholeness

Preview: "Time" and "space" are concepts humans have needed until now to make sense of life on Earth, but they are false concepts when measured against a higher perspective. The predictions about the "end of time" that have always frightened us are not about doom and destruction, but about humankind's beginning to transcend its limiting understanding. The Brotherhood's assignment is to help us do this.

Today we will talk of the end of time—and the beginning of wholeness.

The many predictions about the end of the reckoning of time have worried mankind since the onset of recorded history, for in such a notion is encapsulated the thought of doom. There has always been a dread of the end of everything, as if there were no way to continue after such a boundary. We wish to change that dread into a new perception or awareness, however, because the end of time does not mean the end of everything, but a new way of reckoning. Time itself is a construct devised to shape the perception of Earth life as linear, as proceeding from one thing to another, as cause and effect. This notion is as unreal as the equally useful idea of space as meaning linear location within which causality takes place.

Life on Earth needs such concepts to realize its progression from one stage of evolution or awareness to another. Without these twin constructs, life would be vague, empty of meaning, and seem like a vast, unmanageable mess, neither organized nor sensible. It would be difficult, indeed, for earthly creatures to make sense of anything that happened to them if they had neither a notion of a place in which the occurrence took place, or a framework of when it happened. Thus time and space were devised to lend form its quality of being, its structure.

Now is the time to transcend this misleading format. It is time for time to be overcome. The end of time is upon you, not because time itself will no longer be needed, but because you will begin to see time for what it is—a meaningful construct that is rapidly outgrowing its usefulness. You will begin to realize that time is eternal and you are forever; that the boundaries of time and space are easily overcome by the application of thought; and that the true new age will entail this application of thought and conscious awareness to all forms, including travel, the present, and your identity. It is really this that will describe the end times as the beginning of the true cosmic human.

What we speak of is developing, and will not be seen instantly in your present lives. But, as it appears on the planet, it will supersede the older ledgers of historical record and begin to replace these with a totally new awareness, the elevated awareness of your cosmic history—a history that transcends both space and time. You shall begin to believe in yourselves as neither here nor present, but as forever and everywhere or non-locational. The need for the construct known as time shall be replaced by another awareness altogether, which will usher in the new human—known to itself as truly as aspect of God.

Amen. We await it, and are assigned the job of helping its introduction and manifestation.

We bid you farewell for now.

✶

Postscript

The Process of Channeling

The process of channeling isn't difficult for me. I just sit at a desk, by my computer, or in a comfortable chair, and make sure I have something with which to capture whatever comes through – a pen and notepad, a tape recorder, or best of all, a computer (because I learned years ago to type with my eyes shut). I have to clear all thoughts from my mind – not the easiest task, but one well learned through years of meditating – and wait receptively until I hear them say something.

It's a bit like logging on!

Sometimes I'll ask a question or relay a client's question; sometimes a magazine publisher will give me an upcoming issue's theme; and sometimes I just need a message to help me through my own confusion. In this sense, the Brotherhood "performs" on demand. Usually, the first words I hear are in the nature of "We are here," and I know it will all soon flow. They are always appreciative of being given a platform to speak, and are generous in their thanks. They make things very easy for me: their messages are always well composed, with a beginning, middle, and end, and with a pertinent answer to any question. Some questions are answered vaguely, though, so as to avoid removing an individual's karmic task regarding free will and choice.

I sit to the side and listen. I'm completely there. I'm not "possessed." I'm present but I'm relaying. Words or actual phrases appear in my mind. If I have any problem repeating what I hear, everything stops dead, almost as if they are insisting that I say what they're giving me. Once I surrender to their wishes, it flows again. As I said, it has a beginning, middle, and end, and when it ends, that's it.

No, weird voices do not come out of me! It's always my voice, though the style of the language isn't my own. The pacing is slower, more phrase by phrase. The Brotherhood tells me they search my vocabulary to find appropriate words – if I don't know a word, they can't use it. Even so, some word choices have left me running to the dictionary!

The earliest messages seemed more obscure, but over the course of receiving these channelings, I've found that they've become clearer in meaning as the Brotherhood uses better sentence structure and more accessible vocabulary – or perhaps it's because I've gotten to be a more accomplished recipient!

I don't think the process can be taught. Many have asked me to do so; many yearn for the ability. I think it comes as a gift of spirit. Partly, it manifested after many years of spiritual practice – meditating, learning to still the mind and be present *between* one's thoughts for longer and longer periods. Then there were the many times I'd find myself in an altered state, perhaps dancing, and connecting with spirit; at such times I'd fervently ask to serve the universe and be used by the Divine Force for only the highest purpose. Also, I worked on the concept of surrender of the egoistic self.

Once, decades ago, I had a profound dream: two Tibetan

lamas sat hovering over my head, silently working on my mind. I was imploring them, "When?!" They were sending me the answer telepathically: "We're going as fast as we can!" When I awoke, I found this hysterically funny– I was impatient even in my spiritual goals!

Lastly, there are horoscopic patterns that predispose one to this ability. Before her recent death, I corresponded with one of the contemporary colossi of astrology, Lois Rodden – who'd written an article about her research into the markers of channeling ability found in certain horoscope charts – because I'd found nine of these markers in my chart. She acknowledged that this was rare, and that it certainly confirmed her research.

I'm like a receiver, a telephone, a relay system. I repeat the words I'm hearing. I log on, and they transmit.

The Brotherhood's messages never sound paraphrased or like clichés; they always seem distinctive and original. And it's such an easy way to write! They do all the work – consistently, easily, and with a sense of humor.

Their name itself is both a genuine indicator of their purpose and their lineage, and a play on words. My husband's an electrician and a member of the electrician's union, the International Brotherhood of Electrical Workers; they deliberately chose their moniker as a pun that I'd get!

The information comes through as though previously prepared, with its own agenda and offering concepts that often take me by surprise.

In a way, it's very hard to be a "receiver" – not hard in the physical process but in the sense of giving up control and just allowing. As an organized and levelheaded person, it's kind of scary to hear something like "Five Rules..." and not know if five sensible points will follow! What if nothing follows? Or only four items? What if what follows makes no sense to the prior setup? It's like stepping off a cliff, hoping there's a net below.

On the other hand, if I hesitate to relay the words that have just been given, all comes to a halt and I can't get the flow of words to continue. Surrender is demanded. It's a lesson in trust.

After having clairaudiently received such channeled messages for my family, clients, others, and myself for more than six years, friends began imploring me to produce a book of the Brotherhood's teachings. Everyone had opinions on how to proceed: have an outline and cover certain topics; answer specific questions about today's world; feature a compilation of messages given to clients and others; etc.

It seemed like a good idea, and I wasn't reluctant, but when I tried to start, I wasn't getting the go-ahead from these spiritual guides – that intuitive green light – and so I was hesitant to begin. Probing further, it was revealed that the Brotherhood's main objection seemed to be resistance to a commercial purpose as the basis for the book. Now, as a writer I'm as hopeful as the next guy of producing the newest bestseller, but I had to face the fact that my guides had a much more elevated agenda. If I could just stop trying to "push the river," maybe everything would start to flow.

Finally, once I'd totally surrendered to the Brotherhood and allowed them to decide what, if anything, would come through, I got my green light.

By Chapter Four, I began to realize that there seemed to be a curriculum unfolding in this transmitted material. My summaries, printed herein as "Previews," were an attempt to decipher it.

The world, primed by wars, turmoil, and suffering, and also via the media and the Internet, is ready to think globally and realize how similar and human we all are, that we're truly One.

All of that was preparation (high school); now we're entering college, and are being taught by our professors! There are many channels receiving such teachings nowadays.

The very act of receiving this material has changed my world! For example, the other day I was worrying about the future, going through some habitual financial worries, when suddenly I remembered the control-of-emotion, control-of-thoughts messages. I promptly stopped the worrying in mid-thought and went straight to another concept: let everything happen as it may; then, as things occur, simply adjust any responses in a more positive way!

Just like that, my mood changed, peace descended, and I've stayed remarkably worry-free for the most part since.

Much of this material – everything through Chapter Eleven – was received before "9/11."*

At first, I couldn't think at all about channeling this book, or doing much of anything! Like everyone else, I was in shock. Then, I began to feel an urgency to write – but only to write an article that would explain my thoughts on the event, and its larger meaning from the cosmic perspective. Much energy and effort went into that article, and it was successfully completed and published.†

But even as I was spending hours writing it, there was a day I wondered if the book's material would still come through, if there were still a book at all. So, after about four months, I tried receiving, and the continuity of it was reinstated just as though there'd never been any interruption. They're still here, I realized, and it's still flowing. Time as we know it doesn't exist "up there."

The message that came through for Chapter Twelve was about Fear, Pain, and Sorrow!

The older message was always to reject worldly things, or to remove yourself from the world, in order to find your divine self, but the most powerful concept in this material is a different

---

*Number eleven in numerology, is a "master number."

†"A Final Look Back (& Forward): The Metaphysical Reason Behind the Terrorist Attacks", *Dell Horoscope*, May 2002, archived on my Web site, www.WisdomsGame.com.

take on why we're here. It's that the reason we come here is we had a desire, that desire is manifested in this lifetime, and we're going to play it out as a game. This game will probably bring us suffering, but eventually, if we get the strategy right, we can play it and find joy.

Recently, I was driving along, thinking about Hamlet's soliloquy, "To be or not to be," and that in today's world there really is a new vision, a new concept that's being very strongly given, taught, and communicated to us. All the fear buried in Hamlet's "to sleep, perchance to dream" arises from that era – that when you die, there might be nothing, or there might be nightmare afterward – hell. That's what stays his hand from suicide; that's what the speech is about.

And we now have a whole new message. Even John Edward's television show, Crossing Over, is giving masses of people the understanding that there's communication with the dead, and that something outlives the physical that doesn't sound hellish. That's a very important notion: that we, as an era, an age, are being shown a new light.

Section Two

Recap of Messages
Previews Revisited
The Five Rules of Playing Life's Game

Previews Revisited

1. Wisdom teaches that, while temporary pain is normal, continual suffering over its cause isn't necessary. We can instantly change our thoughts to take things more lightly.

2. You are spirit inside matter—this trick required the sacrifice of *knowing* your real power. You okayed this for one reason: to learn wisdom. There's only one way to get to it: to accept suffering, which is the gift that turns pure but boring spiritual existence into challenging and purposeful life. The struggle of growing is what life's all about. Enjoy it!

3. Higher beings have needs too—primarily, to seek ever-deeper awareness. One of the best ways is to play the game of physical life. The rules of this game demand the acceptance of being small and limited. Smallness and limitation govern the physical universe, and are desirable strategies because their nature provides the richest field of experience.

4. Emotions are our albatross, but we willingly accepted their burden as the strategic challenge required to play

the game of life, a game devised to cause growth. Up to now, we weren't aware that life was a game. But the basis of the Age of Aquarius is to remember our higher nature, our participation in this creation. The time has come—the "End Times"—to change the way the game is played. A new game is developing.

5. Spirit is always helping matter evolve into the state where material perfection is realized, and whose currency is wisdom. Perfection has been realized many times but is always a little different, so the cycle goes on. In the present cycle, the computer will play a key role: it will allow for the development of a global mind to handle the rapid changes and yearnings that always herald higher attainment.

6. To be dissatisfied is to feel deeply your spiritual nature and its need for constant expansion. Knowing this means you won't blame yourself for negative emotions, but will awaken to the rules of playing the game of life successfully.

7. The spiritual state of being is heaven, and we remember it deep down as "home." It always pulls us, making us use various, often destructive, strategies to cope with life's inherent unhappiness. But if we understand life as a game based on seeking spiritual bliss while stuck in physical misery, we can learn to play wisely. As player, you choose exactly who you'll be and what you'll bring to the game. You design your individual playing field and your unique tools. You choose to explore different types of experiences.

The special inner light that always accompanies you throughout the game, though seldom recognized, is now very available. Awareness of your power is growing. There's never been a better time to "win."

8. The age-old pain of discontentment with physical existence is about to be replaced by a new standard: discovering your soul's higher purpose and striving to reach it. Defining it will require new methods. Seeking it will alter society. The game of life is being transformed.

9. All who are alive are in school, and shouldn't waste the experience. Use life to learn wisdom of any type, but especially that of learning to be loving. Value even the painful efforts as badges of the struggle toward enlightenment.

10. Some people measure their worth, not against worldly accomplishments, but against how well their choices reflect wisdom and benefit humanity. They don't distinguish between their own good and the world's when taking creative action. These are the people who carry the responsibility for enlightening all of mankind.

11. To reach true spiritual consciousness, there are three "easy" steps: sensing spirit's presence, then overcoming skepticism to digest the teachings being given, and finally, realizing that you are of the very same spiritual nature as your guides. Don't worry if you can't do the steps right away—the opportunity will always beckon.

12. Pain and sorrow—the causes of fear—are necessary to prevent life on earth from seeming like a pleasant but

unreal dream. They are also the required precursors to the most intense joy. Such are the rules of the game of life.

13. A fatalistic, despairing attitude about life is a false concept. We are not helpless and isolated beings, but fragments of the life force of the universe, creating and completing it with our every thought and action.

14. By endlessly recombining the basic material of itself, the universe explores newness. The purpose behind such constant creation is self-knowledge—the same as humanity's purpose. Whether the design is called the Divine Plan or the mandate of nature, humanity is the stage of the overall creation where the divine realizes itself.

15. During the long journey from spirit into full human form (i.e., greatest density), light had to be covered up and weighted down, resulting in darkness and all it entailed. Darkening of the light inevitably brought pain and ignorance. In turn, life's dark emotions motivated a quest for the truth of one's nature, giving clear purpose to the suffering. Now that the peak of density and suffering has been reached, the transformation of reawakening has happily begun.

16. The only place where duality exists is in the mind, a funny paradox, because mind is the tool to perceive duality, and thus will persist in concealing the truth. This is the complex but playful part of life's game. To solve the puzzle and win the game is to overcome the illusion and return to oneness, which will produce joy. Meanwhile, all your creations, good or bad, are serving the purpose of

fashioning the world while teaching greater awareness.

17. Bliss (complete joy and peace) is the spiritual (non-physical) state. It can be reached momentarily by using thoughts to leap directly out of pain and into transcendent awareness, an act that takes one out of form and back to one's true spiritual state. But to be alive and yet remain in bliss is a challenge; the whole rousing game of life is to figure out how to stay in bliss while staying in form. To find heaven—that is, to leave life's pain—without dying, is to realize this primary chosen test and achieve it.

18. For those who might have difficulty with the notion of other realms of existence, consider this: thought is just such a different realm, a place where the laws of the physical plane don't hold up. But the more it's delved into, the more we can know our true nature and God's.

19. Don't fear the end of time. Humanity will continue to be and to evolve into something closer to ideal spiritual form. All the Earth's history has been spent on humanity's realization, and God won't allow it to be tossed aside, so work diligently at creating the future's design in the best way for yourself and for the world.

20. False ideas about mankind's fate and relationship to God, as well as the nature of God, have arisen as responses to our long history of becoming intelligent and self-aware. We have finally come close to seeing ourselves as God-like creators, which is the meaning of life and the reason the universe came into being. Cultivating beings who

know themselves as God is what universes always do, but reaching full development always includes reaching the ability to self-destruct, too. Not to worry, though! We're not ready to obliterate ourselves yet because we're not finished with the job.

21. "Time" and "space" are concepts humans have needed until now to make sense of life on Earth, but they are false concepts measured against a higher perspective. The predictions about the "end of time" that have always frightened us are not about doom and destruction, but about humankind's beginning to transcend its limiting understanding. The Brotherhood's assignment is to help us do this.

The Five Rules of Playing Life's Game

Rule #1: Remember your greater self at all times while in form.

Rule #2: See all that is happening to you as part of your bargain, not as the trap or mess you have fallen into.

Rule #3: Remember that no one else but you has devised the very traps, messes, and dilemmas that are causing you so much pain and discomfort.

Rule #4: Remember the methods for changing every problem into its opposite.

And Rule #5 (for now): Use your trump card, your ace in the hole, which is none other than the control of thought.

Please use this order form to order additional copies or send a gift of **Wisdom's Game**

No. of books ordered @ $12.95 each _____

☐ *Please put me on your book catalog mailing list.*

Shipping & handling charges: $3.00 USPS or $6.00 UPS or priority mail, plus $1.00 for each additional book.

Subtotal: $ _____

California 7.25% sales tax $ _____

Shipping & handling $ _____

Total: $ _____

Ship to:

Name _____

Address _____

_____

City _____

State _____ Zip _____

Name _____

Address _____

_____

City _____

State _____ Zip _____

☐ Check enclosed

Charge to:

☐ VISA ☐ MasterCard

☐ AmEX ☐ Discover

Card No. _____

Expiration Date _____
Authorized cardholder signature

_____

Daytime phone _____

Gift Card Information

To:

From:

Send your orders to:
Cypress House • 155 Cypress Street • Fort Bragg, CA 95437
or call 1-800-773-7782 • Fax credit card orders to 707-964-7531
or visit our website at www.cypresshouse.com
For consultations, products, and articles by Judi Thomases, or for more information, please visit www.WisdomPath.com.
Or visit www.WisdomsGame.com for information about the Brotherhood of Light Workers' ongoing offerings.
Thank you!